D0809154

The Federal Manager's Guide to Discipline

Second Edition

By

Dennis K. Reischl

and

Ralph R. Smith

FPMI Communications, Inc.
3322 South Memorial Parkway
Suite 40, Building 400
Huntsville, Alabama 35801

(205) 882-3042
Fax (205) 882-1046

Federal Manager's Guide to Discipline
(Second Edition)
Printed in April 1991

ISBN 0-936295-19-8

Table of Contents

Chapter One

Basic Concepts Used in Disciplinary Actions

Chapter Two

Deciding Whether to Take Disciplinary Action

Chapter Three

Selecting a Penalty

Chapter Four

Special Considerations in Taking Disciplinary Actions

Chapter Five

Effectively Dealing with Employees

Chapter Six

Taking Action Based on Performance

Chapter Seven

Handling Grievances and Appeals

Chapter Eight

Practical Advice

Preface

Have you ever been involved in a disciplinary action that was overturned? If you have, you already know that it is one of the most discouraging things that can happen to a manager or supervisor. After having mustered your courage and gone to all the trouble of proposing and carrying out discipline in hopes of correcting a problem, having the action overturned later can be a particularly demoralizing experience.

The most unfortunate aspect of this is that in the majority of cases, the ending could have been avoided by understanding and applying a few simple methods used in handling disciplinary situations. And that is where *The Federal Manager's Guide to Discipline* will help you become a more effective supervisor.

A Method To Our Madness

This book is written for one purpose: to provide Federal managers and supervisors with the practical information they need to use the disciplinary process effectively.

We have done several things to accomplish this. First, we have boiled down the basic ideas and unwritten rules behind the Federal Government's personnel system into plain English.

Second, we have used practical examples to explain how to deal with the typical problems Federal supervisors face on the job. This will give you a concrete picture about putting a particular idea or approach into action.

Third, we have included a summary of the important points covered at the end of each chapter. These points are there to provide a quick way to refresh your memory on key items, not to provide a substitute for reading the chapters. We strongly recommend reading the whole book, at least once, so that you get a complete picture of how the disciplinary process works under the Federal personnel system.

Finally, we have included practical insights gathered during the authors' more than 25 collective years experience in dealing with discipline in the Federal service. Consequently, what follows is not based just on academic theory or "what the book says," but on real life in the Federal Service. We are certain that you will find it informative and helpful.

Introduction

As a supervisor or manager you know that taking disciplinary action against an employee is not an easy or pleasant task. For that reason, many Federal supervisors try to avoid using discipline if at all possible. Among the reasons supervisors often give for avoiding the use of disciplinary action are the following:

★ Taking disciplinary action is time-consuming, and my time is already tight.

★ The procedures required for taking action are complicated, and it is easy to make mistakes.

★ A disciplinary action may be over-turned if a grievance or appeal is filed, making me look bad to senior management.

★ Taking action against one person can create hard feelings among employees and create an unpleasant work environment.

★ I do not like conflict, and would rather not confront an employee.

These are all legitimate concerns, of course, and they are bound to enter the mind of any supervisor considering whether to impose disciplinary action. But there are also several other very important things that you need to recognize and think about when considering how to deal with a problem in the workplace:

1. Disciplinary action is an important tool designed to help managers and supervisors maintain an orderly and productive work environment. Properly used, the disciplinary action process will assist employees in correcting unacceptable behavior that may ultimately threaten their jobs.

2. Failing to use disciplinary action to correct inappropriate behavior often leads to more problems for the supervisor, and may harm the morale of those employees who are working according to the rules and requirements of the workplace.

3. If you understand when and how to use disciplinary action properly, you can deal effectively with most of the concerns outlined above.

4. The time and effort you spend to correct problems early is a good investment. To use the words of a popular television commercial of several years ago, "you can pay now"—by taking effective discipline when necessary—"or you can pay later"—in additional problems, decreasing morale and productivity, and loss of respect and authority. Seen in that light, the proper choice of action for a supervisor is a clear one.

Structure of the Book

The purpose of this book is simple: to enable you to use disciplinary action confidently and effectively when necessary. To reach that objective *The Federal Manager's Guide To Discipline* has been organized into three sections:

In the first section, the basic ideas underlying the use of disciplinary action are discussed. These include several important concepts that you need to understand:

    ★ The purpose behind disciplinary action.

    ★ The idea of corrective, progressive discipline, and how it works.

    ★ "Efficiency of the service" and "just cause" and how they apply to you when taking disciplinary action.

The second section of this book deals with the actual steps involved in carrying out a disciplinary action. These include:

    ★ Deciding whether to discipline; and

    ★ Selecting a disciplinary penalty.

Finally, in the third section, you will learn:

    ★ Special considerations to apply in situations involving drug or alcohol abuse.

    ★ How to deal effectively with employees during the disciplinary process.

The Federal Manager's Guide to Discipline will not make you an expert on all details required to initiate and complete the process of taking action against an employee. But it will make you aware of the typical problems and pitfalls you may encounter. A basic understanding of the discipline system will make you a more confident, effective supervisor. It will also provide you with the information you need to discuss disciplinary action with your personnel office and senior management. In short, it will equip you to deal with disciplinary problems confidently and competently, and enable you to be a better manager.

Basic Concepts Used In Disciplinary Actions

Basic Concepts

For the purposes of this book, we will use the term *disciplinary action* to refer to any action taken to correct behavior, from less severe actions—such as letters of warning, reprimands and short suspensions—through major adverse actions such as removal from Federal employment. The personnel specialists with whom you work on such problems will be familiar with the terms used in this process and will be able to provide any additional explanation that may be needed.

The Purpose of Disciplinary Action

The purpose of a disciplinary action is simple: To maintain an efficient, productive and orderly work environment. The ability to take disciplinary action will help meet that objective by providing supervisors and managers a tool that they can use to enforce the rules, regulations, and work requirements that allow the agency to accomplish its mission in an effective and efficient manner.

Fortunately, you will find that it is seldom necessary to actually take disciplinary action against employees. Most employees want to do a good job and willingly abide by established requirements. For the occasional employee who will not abide by the requirements of your agency or activity, fairness to other employees requires that you take effective disciplinary action when circumstances require it.

Knowing that the rules will be enforced through the use of discipline is usually sufficient to discourage inappropriate behavior. That is why disciplinary action—and the knowledge that it will be used to correct unacceptable behavior—serves as a tool for managers to use in maintaining the morale, efficiency and productivity of the workplace.

Corrective, Not Punitive

A second concept you need to understand is that disciplinary action is used to *correct* inappropriate behavior, *not to punish employees*. Disciplinary action should be designed to make an impression on the employee without being unnecessarily harsh. The purpose is to correct the problem, not to punish the employee beyond the action necessary to reasonably ensure that the same conduct will not be repeated.

"For the occasional employee who will not abide by the requirements of your agency or activity, fairness to other employees requires that you have the ability to take effective disciplinary action when circumstances require it."

There are several sources to help you to determine what the appropriate penalty is for a specific offense. First, the personnel office will be able to advise you on whether similar actions have occurred in the past and, if they have, what actions were taken to correct the problem.

Your agency may also have a "table of penalties" that is designed to provide guidance on what range of penalties are appropriate for various offenses. Also, decisions of third parties (such as the Merit Systems Protection Board or arbitrators) will often provide guidance on how other organizations have handled similar offenses. Again, your personnel office will be able to help you pin down this information and how it will be useful to you.

Progressive Discipline

All Federal agencies—and most private companies—follow an approach called *progressive discipline*. In taking disciplinary action, you will want to follow this same approach. Progressive discipline means that if an employee continues to engage in unacceptable conduct, the actions taken by management to correct the problem will become more severe after each instance.

For example, if an employee is continually late for work, the first step that you might take is counselling, to ensure that the employee is aware of the requirement for coming to work on time. If the employee continues to arrive late, you would usually impose a more severe penalty, such as a letter of warning or a reprimand. Continued violations will

"Progressive discipline: If an employee continues to engage in unacceptable conduct, the action taken by the supervisor to correct the problem will become more severe after each instance."

usually require you to suspend the employee. And, if attendance still does not improve, the employee ultimately may be fired.

Obviously, judgment is required in selecting the appropriate action in each case. In most cases, it is only after a series of progressively more severe disciplinary penalties have failed to correct the employee's behavior that a removal action will withstand review by a third party. The underlying idea is not to punish or "get even" with the employee, but to make it clear that a rule or requirement is important and must be followed.

Note that in some situations, involving particularly serious offenses, *the agency may not be required to use progressive discipline to correct an employee*. In some very serious cases the agency may choose to remove an employee for a first offense. For example, if an employee strikes a supervisor, steals agency property, or commits an act that endangers or harms co-workers, the agency usually may remove the employee without making efforts to correct the behavior. These situations are discussed more thoroughly in Chapter Three.

Conduct Versus Performance

A third important concept that you need to understand is the difference between *conduct* and *performance* problems. **Conduct—or behavior—problems are dealt with very differently from the way that performance problems are handled**. Disciplinary actions are used to correct *conduct problems*, while the performance management system is used to deal with *performance problems*.

The Federal personnel management system—unlike that used in most private sector companies—views misconduct and inadequate performance as two different things. Sometimes it may be difficult to see the dividing line, but in most cases you can do so fairly easily. Here are some short definitions of the two concepts that should help you to see the difference.

> **Misconduct:** *A failure or refusal to comply with a rule, regulation or requirement.*

> **Poor Performance:** *A failure to perform the duties of a position at an acceptable level of quantity, quality or timeliness.*

Rule Of Thumb

A simple rule of thumb will help you to see the difference between them in most situations.

In general, *conduct problems* involve the breaking of a rule, regulation, requirement or direct order. For example, if an employee does not show up for work, or takes agency property for personal use, or refuses to follow a direct order from a supervisor, the behavior would violate rules, requirements or orders, and therefore should be considered a *conduct problem*. Disciplinary penalties, such as a reprimand or suspension, are used to correct such problems.

Performance problems, on the other hand, involve situations in which an employee is performing a job poorly. For example, a typist may make too many typing errors or not turn out the required number of pages per day. A machinist may have too high a scrap/error rate, or an engineering technician may compute numbers incorrectly. These examples are all of poor or unacceptable performance of duties, but not the deliberate breaking of a rule or requirement. Therefore they are *performance problems*. Such problems are usually dealt with through performance counseling, training, performance improvement opportunity periods, and other work improvement efforts.

The situation is likely to constitute misconduct if it involves:

★ *A willful or deliberate action or failure to act.* If an employee is fully capable of carrying out an order but refuses to do so, that is misconduct. On the other hand, if an employee is doing his best to perform a task but lacks the skill, ability or knowledge necessary to do it correctly, the result will be poor performance.

★ *Negligence or inattention is a cause of an unacceptable outcome.* Again, the distinguishing factor is ability to perform work properly. If an employee is fully capable of complying with a requirement but fails to do so out of negligence—such as missing an important deadline that could have been met—it is usually considered misconduct. If an employee is honestly trying to comply with a requirement but fails, that is usually considered poor performance.

★ *A situation involves a rule, regulation or conduct standard.* When an employee breaks a rule—such as missing work without leave—or commits an act contrary to an established conduct requirement—such as engaging in a physical fight, it is misconduct rather than poor performance.

In most cases it is fairly easy to determine whether a problem falls under conduct or performance by using the guidelines outlined above. If the employee is breaking a rule or requirement, it is a conduct problem. If the person isn't doing well on the job, it's usually a performance problem.

But sometimes it may be harder to decide what kind of problem you are facing. For example, if an inventory clerk continues to catalog items incorrectly, it could be because he just doesn't understand the computer system (performance). Or, on the other hand, it could also be because he is coming to work late, leaving early, and not paying attention to his work (conduct). If you are not certain how to label a problem, ask your personnel experts for assistance. You will find that they are very willing and able to provide any assistance they can.

Your Role in Evaluating Conduct

The reason for pointing out the difference between conduct and performance is that you play a central role in evaluating problem situations and determining the appropriate course of action.

If a problem appears to be a conduct situation, you should begin considering necessary disciplinary actions. On the other hand, if the problem is one of performance your role will be considerably different. Rather than considering disciplinary actions, you will likely become involved in identifying additional information, training, coaching or other assistance the employee needs to get fully up to speed. Consequently, it is important that you understand how to identify the type of problem correctly.

The primary purpose of *The Federal Manager's Guide to Discipline* is to provide you with information on how to deal with problems that you have decided involve *misconduct* rather than *performance*.

"Efficiency of the Service" and "Just Cause"

Another concept necessary to understand is the "efficiency of the service" or, as it is sometimes called, the "just cause" standard for taking disciplinary action. For all practical purposes, the two phrases mean the same thing, and the basic idea behind them is as follows:

★ Agency managers and supervisors have the right and responsibility to use discipline to control the conduct of employees.

★ However, discipline can only be imposed where there is a good reason for doing so. This means that the agency must be able to establish that the employee violated some rule or requirement. *Employees are considered innocent until proven guilty.*

Disciplinary Actions

● **Maintain morale and improve behavior**

● **Corrective and not punitive**

● **Progressively more severe**

● **Correct behavior and not performance problems**

● **Taken for just cause**

★ The agency must apply discipline in a fair and reasonable manner. This requires that the discipline be processed in a fair way—by allowing the employee a chance to tell his/her side of the story, for example—and that penalties must be reasonable and consistent with what has been done in similar cases.

It is important to understand these requirements because employees often challenge disciplinary actions through grievance and appeal procedures, claiming that there was not "just cause" for an action or that it does not contribute to the "efficiency of the service." If you have been careful to live up to these requirements in taking discipline, however, chances are excellent that the action will stand. The things you need to do to meet this standard will be discussed in more detail in the following chapters.

Grievances and Appeals

No matter how good your reasons for taking disciplinary action, *the employee has the right to challenge it by filing a grievance or an appeal.* And, in most cases, a grievance or an appeal will be filed.

Whether an employee has a solid basis for appealing your decision is something that is decided in dealing with the grievance itself. In other words, an employee can grieve or appeal first, and find out later if the complaint is legitimate.

You should not take such grievances and appeals personally. Try not to view them as personal challenges to your authority, fairness or ability, although that may be hard to do if the employee says—as they sometimes do—harsh things about your judgment, fairness, or abilities as a manager or supervisor. Look at the entire process as part of doing business as a Federal manager, and not as a personal matter. This will make it easier to keep events in perspective and to avoid making remarks in anger that later can be used to make it appear you may have been biased against the employee.

The responsibility for handling the grievance or appeal is not yours—that belongs to your personnel or legal office. Your primary responsibility will be to answer a grievance filed at the first step of a negotiated grievance procedure, if applicable, and, if necessary, to appear as a witness in any hearing held on the grievance or appeal. Your testimony in a hearing will usually be to give your reasons for taking or recommending disciplinary action.

Key Points

★ The purpose of discipline is to help supervisors and managers to maintain an efficient and productive work environment.

★ Discipline is used to correct unacceptable conduct or behavior, not to punish employees.

★ Conduct or behavior problems involve the breaking of a rule, regulation or other requirement.

★ Performance problems involve an employee's failure to produce work of acceptable quantity, quality or timeliness. Such problems are dealt with differently through the performance management system.

★ In dealing with conduct problems, progressively stiffer penalties are used for additional offenses in order to gain the employee's attention and correct his/her behavior.

★ Corrective, progressive discipline is used in most, but not all situations. Particularly serious violations may result in outright removal.

★ Managers have the right and responsibility to use discipline, but may impose it only for "just cause" or the "efficiency of the service."

★ "Efficiency of the service/just cause" requires both that the agency be able to prove a violation or rule, regulation or other requirement, and that discipline be handled in a fair and consistent manner.

★ An employee has the right to file a grievance or appeal on a disciplinary action. Your role will be primarily to answer the grievance at the first step of the grievance procedure and to give testimony at any hearing that may be held to explain why you took the disciplinary action or recommended that such an action be taken.

Deciding Whether To Take Disciplinary Action

Deciding Whether to Take Disciplinary Action

Picture yourself in the following situation. It's Monday morning and your boss calls you in to tell you that she has heard that one of your employees took agency property home for his personal use over the weekend. The property—it could be anything, from a typewriter to a pickup truck—has been returned, but the boss wants you to check the matter out and recommend what to do.

So what do you do now? What should you "look into?" Should you recommend discipline? If so, how much? What rights, if any, does the employee have? What mistakes should you avoid and how do you recognize mistakes *before* they are made?

Answering these questions is the purpose of this chapter. Any decisions made in taking disciplinary action require an organized approach. This chapter outlines the key steps in the process.

Identify The Problem

Because discipline is used to correct conduct rather than performance problems, a good way to begin is by studying the situation and first deciding the nature of the problem. In this situation, it appears that the employee may have broken a rule or regulation prohibiting the removal and personal use of agency property. If so, that would be a *conduct* problem, and disciplinary action would be the proper tool to correct it.

Get The Facts

You may recall the statement in the initial section of this book that "fair handling" of disciplinary situations is one of the main requirements for meeting the "just cause" standard. An important aspect of "fair handling" is the requirement that management perform a reasonably *full and fair investigation* of a situation *before* deciding upon or carrying out disciplinary action.

"[T]he message is clear: Be careful not to decide what action you are going to take before knowing all of the facts in the case!"

In fact, some arbitrators have overturned disciplinary actions, even though the agency was able to prove a violation of its rules, because management officials did not have that information *before* deciding to impose discipline. While a formal agency investigation is not always required, the message is clear: Be careful not to decide what action you are going to take before knowing all of the facts in the case!

What is required for a "reasonably full and fair investigation?" First the investigator should ask the following questions in order to learn the facts of the case:

▲ What actually happened?

▲ When did it happen?

▲ Where did it happen?

▲ Who witnessed the event?

▲ How did the event or situation occur?

▲ Why did it happen?

▲ Who was accountable for the incident?

Before deciding whether to recommend disciplinary action, carefully consider the facts and evidence that your questions turn up. How do you know that the employee engaged in the conduct in question? Has the employee admitted it? Were there any witnesses? If there is more than one version of the event, which is more believable, and why? If the employee denies having done anything wrong, how strong is the evidence against the employee?

Because discipline is undertaken to correct an employee's conduct, the agency must be able to prove that the employee has done something wrong. *A suspicion that an employee did something wrong is not enough.*

To illustrate, in the example cited above, the agency would have to show that the employee actually took the equipment from the facility before seriously considering disciplinary action. If the agency cannot prove that basic fact, there is no basis for disciplinary action, and any action taken is likely to be overturned if a grievance or appeal is filed.

In short, look before you leap when considering disciplinary action! Don't try to save time and inconvenience by skimping on the initial investigation. The productivity and respect you may lose will exceed any initial savings.

Get The Employee's Side Of The Story

In determining whether management really carried out a reasonably fair investigation, arbitrators and the Merit Systems Protection Board (MSPB) will want to know whether the employee was given a chance to present his or her version of the events leading to the disciplinary action. Most agencies' regulations require that employees be given a chance to respond to a proposed disciplinary action.

Before you decide whether to propose discipline, it is usually a good idea to get the employee's version of events. If the employee is represented by a union, the labor agreement might even *require* you to schedule a face-to-face meeting with the

Look before you leap when considering disciplinary action. It will save problems in the long run.

employee before making a recommendation. If you are not sure whether an employee is covered by such a contract provision, check with your personnel or labor relations experts.

Observe Representation Rights

With regard to unions, there are times when an employee who is in a bargaining unit is entitled to union representation. You need to be aware that if an employee is in a bargaining unit—a group of employees represented by a union—**the employee may be entitled to have a union representative present if you hold any face-to-face meetings with the employee to investigate the situation.**

This is often called the *Weingarten right.* It entitles an employee to representation by a union when the following conditions are met:

▲ The employee is being *questioned by a management representative* in conjunction with an investigation of a problem or incident.

▲ The employee is in a *bargaining unit* of employees represented by a union.

▲ The employee *reasonably believes that disciplinary action may result* from the investigation.

▲ The employee *requests representation.*

Once all of these conditions have been met, an employee is entitled to have a union representative present *if* you are going to continue asking questions.

To use our earlier example, if you were to call the employee in to ask whether he took agency equipment home for use over the weekend, and the employee asked to have a union representative present, you have three choices if he is a member of the bargaining unit:

1. Stop asking questions, end the meeting and make your decision on whatever other information you might have or can get from other sources.

2. Allow a union representative to join the meeting before resuming your questions.

3. Tell the employee that no matter what his answers are, he will not be disciplined, so he has no need of a union representative.

What you choose to do, of course, will depend on the situation. In this example, since you may well want to recommend discipline if the employee has broken an important rule, it is not likely that you will use the third option.

Going back to the example, because you probably would want additional information in this situation, it is most likely that you will select the second choice, and not ask any more questions until a union representative is present. *At that point you could continue asking questions, and getting answers from the employee.*

In these situations, a union representative has the right to ask relevant questions and to make relevant comments to help the employee tell his side of the story, but *does not* have the right to do the talking for the employee, or to prevent you from getting answers to your questions. If you run into a problem, such as a union representative advising an employee not to answer the questions, it is a good idea to call your personnel or labor relations experts for advice and assistance.

A union representative has the right to ask relevant questions and to make relevant comments to help an employee, but does not have the right to answer for the employee or to prevent you from getting answers to your questions.

Note: In some cases, the labor agreement may add other rules you need to know about. For example, some contracts state that the employee must be advised of the right to union representation at the beginning of a meeting that could lead to discipline. Be aware of any such requirements before investigating a possible disciplinary action.

Know The Rules, Regulations, Policies and Union Contract Involved

If you are reasonably certain you can show that an employee has engaged in some conduct that may justify taking disciplinary action, the next step in the decision-making process is to determine if the agency has a rule, regulation or written policy covering the situation. Also be sure to check the applicable union agreement. As a general rule, if there is no rule, regulation or policy that prohibits whatever the employee has done, discipline is not justified. The reason: Discipline is used to correct behavior that violates the agencys rules and requirements. If there is no rule or requirement, there is no basis to discipline an employee.

This *does not* mean that every possible violation by an employee must be covered by a *written* rule or regulation. Some actions are so obviously wrong that no written policy is necessary. For example, your agency may not have a rule against pouring motor oil on a supervisor's desk. Nevertheless, this action by an employee could result in disciplinary action, even without a written policy against it because it is so obviously wrong.

Returning to our example, if the employee admitted taking a typewriter home over the weekend, but the agency has no clear rule against doing so, discipline would probably not be a good idea. A third party, such as an arbitrator, may overturn the penalty. An employee cannot be disciplined for breaking a non-existent rule!

Of course, if there *are* rules or regulations that cover the situation—such as an agency regulation prohibiting personal use of Government property — you should get a copy of them. Read them over carefully before deciding whether to go any further, and ensure that a copy is included in the disciplinary file that will later be used to support any action taken.

Check to See if the Rules Have Been Communicated and Enforced

By this point you are probably thinking that your decision should be clear. If you can show that the employee took the equipment home for his personal use and there is a clear rule against doing so, you will surely be able to use discipline. Many disciplinary actions built on this basis are overturned or reduced, however. Why? Usually because the management officials involved failed to consider two other important questions.

> **Question #1**: Was this rule communicated to employees, or, if not, is the offense so obvious that they could be expected to know about it without being told?

> **Question #2:** Has this rule been consistently enforced in the past, and if not, were employees told that it was going to be enforced before this incident?

One of the most frequent reasons disciplinary actions are overturned is because employees are able to show that they were never told of the rules or regulations. And in disciplinary action, ignorance of the rules *is* an excuse. Generally, there has to be some evidence that employees were told of a rule or knew about it before discipline can be taken.

A rule can be communicated in any of several ways, including posting on bulletin boards, explaining it during orientation sessions or employee meetings, or directly telling employees about it during staff meetings. But unless a rule is obvious, management usually must be able to show that it did something to let employees know about it before imposing discipline.

In most situations, such as those listed in the standard schedule of disciplinary penalties, it will be easy to show that the rule exists and is well-known. But in less common situations, it may be necessary to do a little digging, or to have the personnel office do some digging for you.

If our weekend typist could reasonably claim that he had never heard of the rule against using agency property for personal business, there is not going to be a solid basis for discipline unless the agency can demonstrate that the rule does exist, and that the employee should have been aware of it.

Consistent Enforcement

Furthermore, if the employee can show that the rule has not been consistently enforced, regardless of whether it was communicated to employees, disciplinary action is almost sure to be overturned. Again, the reason is simple: if the rule has not been enforced, the employee can reasonably claim that he did not think it was in effect any longer, or he would not have acted as he did! A simple, effective defense.

So in the sample case, if the employee was able to point out that you or other supervisors had allowed others to take typewriters—or pickup trucks—home for their personal use without disciplining them, chances are you could not impose discipline in this case either.

This *does not mean* that a rule can never be applied if management has not been consistently enforcing it. But it *does mean* that employees must be clearly warned that it will be enforced before imposing discipline on anyone for breaking it.

So if a rule has not been applied consistently and you want to start enforcing it, you should clearly advise employees that:

1. The rule will be applied as of a specific date; and

2. Failure to comply with the rule will lead to discipline.

Making The Decision

By now you may be getting the impression that deciding whether to discipline an employee is a lot of work. If so, you're right. It is a lot of work! But if you do not put in the effort to answer the questions outlined in this chapter, you will be running a

much higher chance that your efforts to correct unacceptable conduct will not pass muster once a grievance or appeal is filed.

Once you can answer the key questions discussed
above, you should be in a good position to confidently make a decision. For example, if after checking
out the situation handed to you by the boss at the
beginning of this chapter, you found that...

> a. The employee *did* take agency equipment
> home for personal use;
>
> b. There *is* an agency rule against doing so;
>
> c. The rule is contained in the employee
> handbook and explained to all employees
> during their orientation;
>
> d. Other employees have been disciplined
> for breaking the rule;

...you would be able to confidently recommend that
some corrective action be taken to resolve the situation. If one or more of these elements is missing,
however, discipline may be inappropriate.

Role of the Personnel Office

Although imposing disciplinary action is a lot of
work, your job will be made easier by the personnel
experts your agency employs to help and advise
you. Here are some of the things you can reasonably expect them to do:

1. Helping you find the particular rules or regulations that may apply to a situation.

2. Helping you to find out when and how a rule may have been communicated to employees, such as during basic employee orientation.

3. Helping you to find out whether a rule has been enforced with discipline in the past.

4. Helping you to determine whether discipline would be likely to withstand the challenge of a grievance or appeal.

5. Helping you to decide whether to impose discipline.

6. Helping you to write up a disciplinary action and meet the technical requirements set up in agency regulations and those issued by the Office of Personnel Management (OPM).

7. Helping you determine which penalty should be used to correct the problem. (This is considered in more detail in the next chapter.)

There are a few more points you should be aware of in seeking help from your personnel office. First, as the list points out, it is important to remember that the personnel specialists are there to help *you* make decisions, not to make them for you. Keep in mind that although the personnel office can provide advice and guidance, the final decision of whether to impose discipline is always up to you. Feel free to ask for help from the personnel office, and listen carefully to their advice, but do not expect to give up your role as the decision-maker in this process. After all, it is *your problem*, not theirs.

Considerations in Disciplinary Actions

- **Investigation results**

- **Observing representation rights**

- **Evidence of wrongdoing**

- **Applicable rules or regulations**

- **Communicating rules to employees**

- **Consistent enforcement**

In short, personnel officials can be extremely helpful in dealing with disciplinary situations. So stay in touch with them, and if there is something that you do not understand, or there seems to be a problem, do not hesitate to keep asking questions until you get a satisfactory answer.

Key Points

★ Supervisors and managers are primarily responsible for deciding upon and carrying out disciplinary action.

★ Many disciplinary actions are overturned or modified either because the agency cannot prove actual wrongdoing, or because a rule was not known to employees and enforced properly, or because the discipline was not carried out in a fair manner.

★ Most problems can be avoided by taking a few simple steps before deciding upon or imposing discipline. They are:

- Investigate the facts first;

- Get the employee's side of the story;

- Allow employees represented by a union to have representation during the investigation;

- Check to see whether there is a rule, regulation or policy that covers the situation;

- Find out whether the rule has been communicated to employees and enforced in the past.

★ The personnel office is available to provide substantial help in investigating a situation, determining whether to discipline, and actually carrying out a disciplinary action.

Selecting
A Penalty

Selecting a Penalty

After going through the steps outlined in Chapter Two, if you determine that an employee has violated a rule or requirement and you feel that some corrective action is necessary, the next step is to decide what specific disciplinary penalty to use. You have several options available.

Options

As you can see from the list below, there is a range of possible actions you can take to correct a problem, from oral reprimands and warnings through removal from the Federal service. Later in this chapter you will learn how to narrow the range of choices. To begin, however, you need to know what the various penalties are and how they work.

Possible Penalties

★ Oral reprimand or warning

★ Written reprimand

★ Suspension of 14 calendar days or less

★ Suspension of more than 14 calendar days

★ Reduction in grade

★ Removal from the Federal service

Oral Reprimand/Warning

As the name implies, an oral reprimand or warning consists of a supervisor telling an employee that particular conduct or behavior is unacceptable and will not be tolerated. In most agencies oral reprimands and warnings are *not* considered a formal disciplinary action. Nevertheless, you may want to keep a personal record of the conversation for later reference, since there will not be a formal notation of it in the employee's official file.

An oral reprimand or warning is the mildest form of corrective action and, in many cases involving minor infractions or a first offense, it is enough to solve the problem. Under the concept of progressive discipline, an oral reprimand or warning is often the first step supervisors take to deal with a problem, and in many cases it is all that will be necessary to correct the problem to your satisfaction.

Unlike more severe actions, there are few, if any, procedural steps that a supervisor must follow in orally reprimanding an employee. As in any disciplinary or corrective action, however, it is wise to check with the personnel office if you are not sure whether any specific procedures are required by agency regulations or a union contract. Even though the corrective action is not a severe one, failure to follow procedural requirements can turn even a minor corrective action into an emotional tug-of-war between you and the employee.

Written Reprimand

A written reprimand is a formal letter to an employee outlining specific unacceptable conduct and usually stating that such conduct will not be tolerated in the future. Often such letters of reprimand specifically note that further misconduct will result in more severe disciplinary action.

Unlike oral warnings, written reprimands are considered a formal disciplinary action, and normally a copy of the letter is entered into the employee's official personnel folder for a specified period of time, usually for a period of 1 to 3 years. While it is in the employee's folder it may be taken into account for a variety of purposes, and may also affect future personnel actions.

Suspension of 14 Calendar Days Or Less

A suspension from duty involves an employee being formally directed to remain away from work for a specified period of time, without pay.

Because the employee loses pay and any differentials that would have been earned on such days, suspensions are obviously more severe than oral or written reprimands. In addition, suspensions are *permanently* recorded in an employee's official personnel folder, and may be taken into account in later personnel actions. Therefore, they are a more severe disciplinary action.

Technically, a 14-day suspension from duty is the most severe *disciplinary action* that can be taken.

That is because Federal regulations refer to longer suspensions, reductions in grade and removals from the service as *adverse actions*. For the purposes of this book, *any* action taken to correct unacceptable conduct or behavior is called a disciplinary action.

Suspensions For More Than 14 Calendar Days

Suspensions for more than 14 days are basically the same as shorter suspensions, except that the employee is away from work for more days and loses more pay. Longer suspensions are obviously more severe than short ones. More important, they are often a signal to the employee that another violation of the rules may result in removal. In addition, the procedural requirements for imposing a suspension of more than 14 days are somewhat different.

Reduction In Grade

This penalty is exactly what it sounds like—moving an employee into a lower grade. For example, reducing a WG-11 Electrician to a WG-9 Electrician, or a GS-5 Clerk/Typist to a GS-4 Clerk/Typist, with a resulting loss in pay rate. Although it is rarely used in disciplinary situations, it is sometimes appropriate, such as situations involving negligence that may endanger other employees. Chances are you will never become involved in using this penalty to correct conduct, although you may see it applied to solve a *performance problem* where an employee is unable to perform the duties of a higher level job.

Removal From The Federal Service

This is the most severe disciplinary action that can be taken. It is only used when:

1. A first offense is so serious that the agency has no interest in correcting an employee, such as physical assault on a supervisor or theft of agency property; or

2. When steadily more severe disciplinary penalties have not succeeded in correcting an employee's conduct, and the agency concludes that further corrective action is unlikely to be effective.

Removal is often considered the workplace equivalent of "capital punishment," and therefore you must look for strong proof of wrongdoing and a clear indication that the employee has been given a reasonable chance to correct his behavior before this drastic step is taken. In short, although many Federal employees are removed for misconduct every year, it is not a penalty to be used without very good cause and careful thought.

Factors To Consider In Selecting A Penalty

The various penalties discussed above provide a list of the various things you *could* do to correct unacceptable conduct, but which of them *should* you use in a particular situation? Remember that, as part of the "just cause" standard, you are required to apply discipline in a fair, reasonable and consistent manner. What makes one penalty more or less fair or reasonable than another? And does "consistent" mean that you must take exactly the same action for the same offense every time? Fortunately, there are a few simple questions you can ask that will help you to reach an answer to this question.

What Does The Penalty Guide Say?

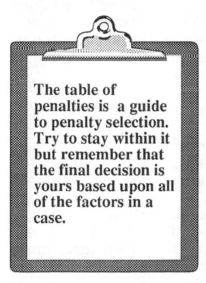

The table of penalties is a guide to penalty selection. Try to stay within it but remember that the final decision is yours based upon all of the factors in a case.

Many agencies have a document or regulation that is called a "penalty guide," "table of penalties" or something similar. Regardless of what it is called, this document describes the various offenses that are prohibited by agency policies. It also provides guidelines for the range of penalties managers should consider for a particular offense.

Often the range of penalties is keyed to the number of times a particular offense has been committed. For example, for a first offense of unauthorized absence from work a penalty guide might suggest penalties ranging from a reprimand to a 5-day suspension. For a second offense it might suggest a 5-to 14-day suspension; and for a third offense, a 14-day suspension to removal. In most situations your selection of a penalty will fall within the guidelines, unless there   are unusual reasons for exceeding them.

If your agency uses one, a penalty guide is a good place to start because it will give you an idea of the range of penalties to consider. As you can see, even within these established guidelines there is usually a great deal of room for the supervisor to select a specific penalty. Sometimes, in fact, the stated range of possible penalties for an offense may run from reprimand all the way to removal! The question then becomes, how do you select a proper penalty within the range of discretion given by the table of penalties? Asking yourself the following questions will assist you in finding the answer.

What Is The Employee's Record?

The reason penalty guides provide a range of possible penalties for offenses is to allow managers to apply their best judgment based on various important considerations. One of those considerations is the employee's past record, including length of service with the agency. To illustrate, if a 20-year employee of the agency with a clean disciplinary record commits a first offense of unauthorized absence from work, it is likely that the penalty will be chosen from the low end of the range. On the other hand, if a 2-year employee of the agency with several other disciplinary offenses already on his record commits the same offense, he may be removed—even though this may be his first unauthorized absence! The reason for the difference is that the accumulated disciplinary record may indicate that he is not going to become a satisfactory employee regardless of the discipline taken against him. In short, both the employee's *length of service* and *disciplinary record* can be important considerations in selecting a penalty.

What Is The Impact Of The Offense On The Agency?

Consider the example of the 20-year employee involved in a first offense of unauthorized absence or absence without leave (AWOL). Normally, the minimum prescribed penalty would be used in this situation. But if the employee was AWOL for a long period of time, his action may have severely affected the ability of your organization to accomplish its job. It may have also affected other employees by requiring the cancellation of their approved leave requests. In this case, a more severe penalty may be appropriate because of the *impact upon the organization.*

In other words, in determining a fair, reasonable and appropriate penalty, you should consider the results, or likely results, of the employee's offense. For example, was someone harmed or placed in danger because of the employee's actions, and what was the actual or probable cost to the Government as a result of the employee's conduct?

What Is The Nature Of The Employee's Job?

The penalty selected also may be more or less severe depending on the *nature of the employee's work*. For example, a security guard who falls asleep while guarding top secret documents would be more severely disciplined than one who falls asleep guarding a parking lot.

Similarly, a tax specialist employed by the Internal Revenue Service would probably be more severely penalized for cheating on his taxes than would a welder employed in a Navy shipyard, because of the nature of their jobs and the different missions of their employers.

What Penalties Have Been Applied In Similar Situations?

A personnel specialist can be particularly helpful in advising you as to how similar situations have been handled previously. For example, she can probably tell you what penalties have been applied when an employee has committed a second offense of leaving work early but has an otherwise clean record. Such information is helpful in letting you know whether the penalty you have in mind is within the range of penalties normally imposed by your agency.

As a general rule, if a situation is similar to others that have come up, the penalty you select should be similar, unless there are other significant differences, such as the employee's record or much greater impact on the agency or other employees.

The idea behind the requirement for consistency is not to strap your hands in dealing with problems, but to ensure fairness and equal treatment of employees. By requiring that similar misconduct result in similar penalties, all employees are treated fairly and can reasonably know in advance what penalty to expect when engaging in misconduct.

Should The Penalty Be Lighter Than Normal?

Sometimes there are special circumstances connected with an offense which provide a good reason for imposing a lighter penalty than would normally be used in the situation. For example, if an employee struck a supervisor after being provoked by a racial taunt, a less severe penalty might be applied because the supervisor shared the blame for the incident. Similarly, an employee who was absent without leave because of serious family problems might be dealt with less harshly than someone who was AWOL to go fishing.

Is The Offense Related To A Drug Or Alcohol Problem?

In some instances, an employee's behavior stems from a drug or alcohol-related problem and in such cases a different approach to discipline may be required. If an employee claims that his misconduct is the result of drug or alcohol problems, or if you have other reasons to suspect that this is the case, several other things must be considered before you impose a disciplinary action. These considerations are covered in detail in Chapter Four.

Role of the Personnel Specialist

The personnel experts in your agency can be essential to you in determining what disciplinary penalty to use in a specific situation. A personnel specialist can help by getting the relevant information from the penalty guide, finding out what has been done in similar situations in the past, letting you know how arbitrators and the Merit Systems Protection Board consider penalties for the offense involved, and serving as a sounding board for your ideas on what to do. In short, they can help keep you on track, save you a lot of time, and provide all the support you need to make a decision that you will be comfortable with and can explain later if a grievance or appeal is filed.

Key Points

★ Managers and supervisors have a considerable amount of room to decide upon the appropriate penalty to correct a conduct or behavior problem.

★ Disciplinary penalties can range from oral warnings to removal from the Federal service.

★ There are several important factors to consider before selecting a disciplinary penalty. These include:

• The agency's penalty guide;

• The employee's length of service and record;

• The impact of the offense on the agency;

• The nature of the employee's work;

• Penalties that have been applied in similar situations;

• Reasons for imposing a lighter penalty than normal;

• Whether drugs or alcohol might be involved.

★ Personnel experts can be essential in determining an appropriate penalty and helping you to explain and defend your decision.

Special Considerations In Taking Disciplinary Actions

Special Considerations

Drugs, Alcohol and Discipline

Here is a common situation that managers and supervisors encounter in dealing with disciplinary problems. Jill, one of your employees, has had a satisfactory work record during her five years in your organization, but over the past several months she has started coming in to work late, sometimes as much as one hour. At first you said nothing about it, because she has always been a good employee and has put in extra effort when necessary.

When her late arrivals became a habit, you called her aside and reminded her that it is necessary to come to work on time. Jill was apologetic, explained all the problems she has getting the kids off to school on time, and promised to do better. But the situation did not improve. Finally, despite your personal feelings, you gave her a written reprimand, after which she stopped talking to you unless absolutely necessary. After a week of doing better, she began coming in late again—last Monday she arrived two hours late without calling in or offering any explanation. You called her in, asked why she was late—she mumbled something about the traffic—and said you would be proposing a short disciplinary suspension for tardiness.

Today Jill informed you that her tardiness is related to an alcohol problem. What are your options now? Should you go ahead with the discipline? Is Jill now immune to discipline? Do any special procedures apply to an employee with a drug or alcohol problem? If so, what are they?

The Duty Of Reasonable Accommodation

In the Federal service, employees who become dependent upon alcohol or other drugs that affect their performance or conduct are viewed as being "qualified handicapped employees." The importance of this is that "handicapped employees" are entitled to "reasonable accommodation" of their handicapping condition. In these cases, the handicapping condition is, of course, the addiction to alcohol or other drugs.

What does this mean to you? If an employee commits various offenses that you know, suspect, or are told are connected to an alcohol or drug dependency, Federal law and regulations require that the agency make a reasonable effort to accommodate the person's disabling problem.

To get a handle on what reasonable accommodation is all about and how it affects you in dealing with misconduct, there are some basic terms you should know.

▲ A *handicapping condition* is defined by law as any physical or mental impairment that restricts an individual in one or more of life's major activities.

▲ *Reasonable accommodation* is a logical adjustment to a job or the work environment that allows an otherwise qualified person who suffers from a handicapping condition to perform the duties of his or her position.

57

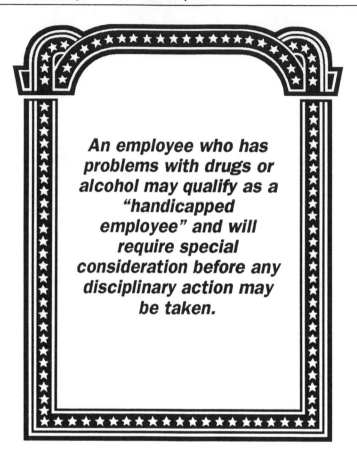

An employee who has problems with drugs or alcohol may qualify as a "handicapped employee" and will require special consideration before any disciplinary action may be taken.

▲ An employee assistance program (EAP) exists to provide help to employees in dealing with personal problems that may be affecting their performance or conduct.

How does this affect you? First, you must be alert to identify factors that may qualify as handicapping conditions in dealing with employees who engage in misconduct. Although a particular physical handicap may be apparent, others are not always so obvious. Nevertheless, if a third party or a court later determines that you should have recognized that an employee's misconduct was rooted in a personal problem—such as alcoholism—any action you take may be overturned. Consequently, you must be reasonably alert to the signs of drug and alcohol dependence, as well as mental impairment.

Second, recognize that failing to provide reasonable accommodation where possible can serve as a basis for overturning any disciplinary or adverse action you may take. Keep an open mind and demonstrate a reasonable willingness to accommodate an employee's efforts to overcome a handicapping condition.

As a practical matter, this generally boils down to the following:

1. In most cases, the agency must attempt to help the employee overcome the handicapping condition of drug or alcohol dependency. It usually does so by referring the employee to an Employee Assistance Program coordinator or other competent professional help. If you suspect an employee's behavior is being affected by drugs or alcohol, *it is your responsibility* to inform the employee of the agency's employee assistance program (EAP) and to offer to help her make contact with it.

You should not tell the employee you suspect drug or alcohol abuse, or attempt to have the employee admit using drugs or alcohol. Informing him of the program and offering assistance if he wants it is sufficient. You do not have to force the employee to accept such assistance and the employee is not obligated to follow your advice.

2. If the employee *does* follow your advice and seeks assistance, "reasonable accommodation" usually turns out to mean that you are required to hold off carrying out discipline if the employee becomes involved in a rehabilitation program and attempts to overcome the problem. So, in our example, if Jill enrolled in a program designed to help her stop drinking, you would have to accommodate her handicap by not suspending her for last Monday's late arrival. In addition, you may also be required to allow her to use sick leave, annual leave, or leave without pay for participation in a rehabilitation program as part of the duty to "reasonably accommodate" her problem. In some cases, misconduct may be so egregious that the alcoholic is removed from the protection of the Rehabilitation Act.

3. *If the employee does not admit the problem*, and fails or refuses to follow your advice, you may go ahead with discipline. To illustrate this, let's change Jill's example. Assume that although she *did not* raise the issue, you suspected that Jill has an alcohol problem. But when you advised her to seek the assistance of the EAP program, she denied any problem and refused to get help. In that situation, you would usually go ahead with the discipline in the hope that the employee will begin to see the handwriting on the wall and take steps to get the situation under control. Discipline and referral can both occur but an employee cannot usually be terminated for the first offense.

4. What if the employee admits the problem, enrolls in an assistance program, but *continues the behavior* that created the problem to begin with? Is she now immune from discipline? *In a word, no.* Reasonable accommodation requires the agency to

cooperate with the employee in an effort to help him beat the problem. It does not mean that managers have to put up with unacceptable conduct indefinitely. If his behavior does not improve, discipline can and should be used to try to help straighten her behavior out.

Also, if an employee does admit to having a problem, she should be given a "firm choice" between participating in a rehabilitation program or facing disciplinary action.

Using Common Sense

Contrary to what you may have heard or expected, dealing with alcohol and/or drug-related problems is not complicated for the operating manager or supervisor. Mostly it requires common sense in dealing with employees. Here are several suggestions you will find helpful if you have to deal with one of these situations.

★ **Keep your eyes and ears open. Do not avoid recognizing a problem.**

In most cases, employees provide hints and clues when they are experiencing a drug or alcohol problem. If they are chronically late, have bloodshot eyes, are sleepy at work, have slurred speech, stumble and weave, or smell of alcohol, the employee probably has an alcohol related problem. You do not have to wait for a disciplinary situation to try and help the employee. You can talk directly with the employee or you may discuss the situation with the EAP counselor first. Either way, manage with your eyes open.

★ Expect denials and non-cooperation.

People who become addicted to drugs or alcohol often deny the problem until confronted with a heavy shock—such as a proposal of discipline or removal. Before that point, despite your best efforts, an employee will probably deny the problem. Until an employee admits there is a problem, your only recourse is to use discipline.

★ Do not expect miracles.

People suffering from an addiction, particularly from alcohol, may not make a perfect recovery without an occasional lapse. Although you have the right and responsibility to require improvement, common sense and an honest desire to help may mean you will have to accept and deal reasonably with an occasional step backward.

In your meeting with the employee, concentrate on conduct or disciplinary problems. It is not the supervisor's role to diagnose drug or alcohol problems.

There is one important exception: if your agency has worked out a "last chance" arrangement with an employee, and he violates the agreement, the best approach is usually to go ahead with the discipline or removal. Otherwise such agreements are worthless, and employees soon come to expect several more "last chances." In effect, they are unlikely to face up to and solve their problems if they do not think you mean what you say.

★ **Use discipline as a tool to help the employee, not as an automatic penalty**.

Some managers and supervisors become overly-rigid in their approach, and apply disciplinary penalties in a mechanical fashion when more flexibility is necessary. For example, if an employee has enrolled in a rehabilitation program, faithfully attended it for a year, and has not been late or absent once during that entire time, an incident of one-hour's tardiness because of a one-night lapse should not automatically result in the next step up the disciplinary schedule. In such a situation, a lesser penalty might be more than sufficient. After all, the point of reasonable accommodation is to attempt to salvage good employees, not to see who can win a game of *Gotcha!* with the employee's job at stake.

★ **Make an honest effort to help, but don't let an unsuccessful employee wreck your work group**.

If good faith efforts to help an employee overcome a problem have not been successful, it may be necessary to fire the employee. Although no one enjoys taking someone's job away, your first responsibility is to the agency and the other employees under your supervision. If an employee's repeated failure to overcome an alcohol or drug problem is placing an undue burden on the rest of the work group, your best bet is to do what is necessary—discipline or remove the problem employee.

★ Do not try to force the employee to visit the EAP counselor.

It is up to the employee to follow through, if he chooses to do so.

★ Do not try to learn what the employee tells the EAP counselor.

This information is confidential unless the employee voluntarily chooses to tell you. In some cases you will, of course learn the nature of the problem if the employee seeks special accommodation or assistance in overcoming it. For example, if the employee seeks leave without pay (LWOP) to attend an alcohol or drug rehabilitation program, you will obviously become aware of the nature of the problem.

★ Do not make referrals except on a job-related basis.

That is, refer an employee to the EAP only if you see an on-the-job problem. Although you may suspect an employee to be an alcoholic, there is no basis for referral to the EAP if the employee is performing at an acceptable level and has not exhibited any conduct problems.

Key Points

★ Discipline for offenses related to drug or alcohol abuse is handled differently than other conduct problems.

★ The agency is required to provide "reasonable accommodation" for the "handicapping condition" of drug or alcohol addiction.

★ Managers and supervisors are responsible for offering "reasonable accommodation" assistance to employees who are known or suspected of having an alcohol or drug dependency problem.

★ Reasonable accommodation of a drug or alcohol problem may include referral to an Employee Assistance Program, enrollment in a rehabilitation program, and allowing leave with or without pay to become rehabilitated.

★ If an employee seeks such assistance discipline is usually held off.

★ If an employee refuses to seek assistance or fails to improve, discipline can and should be used.

★ A common sense, good faith effort by supervisors and managers is necessary to deal effectively with drug and alcohol-related conduct problems.

Effectively Dealing With Employees

Effectively Dealing with Employees

During the disciplinary process, dealing with the employee who is the subject of the disciplinary action will be one of your primary concerns. As a supervisor, you want to ensure that the work of your organization continues to be accomplished with minimal disruption. If not handled properly, the disciplinary action process can create more problems than it solves in your organization. This chapter explains how to minimize the chance of additional problems.

Primary Objective

Remember, the primary objective of the disciplinary process is correcting a problem. With that in mind, it is necessary to approach your dealings with the employee you are disciplining objectively, candidly, and in a professional (i.e. unemotional) manner. This is sometimes the most difficult aspect of the disciplinary process.

Some employees will react strongly and emotionally to your attempts to impose discipline. In many instances, the initial reaction of the employee will be to blame you, co-workers, senior management, or anyone but himself for the situation. Your challenge will be to see beyond the immediate reaction and keep your objective in mind: correcting the problem, *not* winning a battle with the employee.

> # Meeting With An Employee
>
> ---
>
> ● **Explain the problem**
>
> ● **Explain why it is a problem**
>
> ● **Explain what you expect the employee to do to correct the problem**

Set a Professional Tone

From the earliest point in the process, you need to set a calm, constructive and non-emotional tone in your dealings with the employee. When you are first investigating the situation and determining whether discipline is appropriate, avoid emotional outbursts and threats of discipline. Once you allow your relationship with an employee to begin on that footing, it is hard to change it later. It is also difficult to get employees to take a positive attitude toward your attempts to correct their behavior once an emotional, combative tone has been established.

Explain your Reasons for Action

Since the point of taking disciplinary action is to improve the employee's behavior, it is important to let the person know *why* you believe discipline is appropriate. When meeting with the employee to

---

discuss the problem, make your purpose clear. Explain *what* the problem is, *why* it is a problem from your point of view, and *what* you expect the employee to do to resolve the problem to your satisfaction.

It is important to explain the reasons for your dissatisfaction. In some instances, you will find that the employee genuinely did not understand that his actions created a problem for you or why they are a problem. A face-to-face discussion may help resolve this situation quickly.

Outline Future Expectations

It is important to tell the employee what your expectations are because it is important to prevent past mistakes from reappearing in the future. For example, if an employee has been consistently coming to work late, specifically tell the employee that "I expect you to be here by 8:00 a.m." Not telling the employee exactly what you expect may leave an inaccurate impression and create problems for you later—especially if you find it necessary to take disciplinary action.

Provide Reassurance

Discipline is not a pleasant experience for employees. An employee who is disciplined may become resentful and fearful of his future in the organization. If you want a productive, enthusiastic employee, it is in your interest to reassure the person that improving his behavior will end the matter. There are several steps you can take to make this happen.

First, try to end any meetings to discuss your decision to take disciplinary action on a positive note. Reassure the employee that your only interest is in resolving the problem—not in riding their backs or taking further disciplinary action.

Second, offer to help the employee by meeting more frequently or reviewing the situation again on a specific date.

Third, tell the employee that improving his conduct will close the matter and place his career back on track as far as you are concerned.

If you take these small but important steps, you will greatly increase your chances of the employee viewing the disciplinary action in a positive light.

Keep Notes

A final, important piece of advice in dealing with employees during the disciplinary process is to keep notes of *when* you meet with people, *what* was said, and what *things you intend to check out.*

You will find, especially if a grievance or appeal is filed, that keeping track of what was said and what occurred to you during the process will be very helpful. Imagine yourself trying to remember six months later exactly what was said at a particular meeting, and you may see how and why notes can be essential. They are proper, they are useful, and you can only hurt yourself by not keeping them. So why not make the effort?

Key Points

★ Successful corrective discipline requires effective face-to-face dealings with the disciplined employee.

★ The key to effective dealings is setting and maintaining a professional, unemotional tone in all communications with the employee.

★ It is important to explain the reasons for recommending disciplinary action.

★ You should outline your specific expectations for future behavior.

★ Providing reassurance that improvement will place the employee back in good standing is important in fostering a positive attitude toward the discipline.

★ Keep notes of facts, statements, meetings and your thought processes; they may be critical in explaining your actions later.

Taking
Action
Based
On
Performance

Taking Action Based on Performance

You may recall that in the first chapter of this book (see page 15) a distinction was made between actions that involve the *conduct* of an employee and those that concern an employee's *performance*. As noted previously, performance-based actions are treated differently than actions based on conduct. This chapter briefly considers the procedures for taking an action based on unacceptable *performance*.

The Performance Plan

Before taking any action based on performance, it is essential for the employee to have received a performance plan. This plan lists the *job elements* for the employee's position and the *performance standards* for the position. Before taking action against an employee for poor performance, you should check with your servicing personnel office to make certain that the performance plan is sufficiently clear and specific.*

The performance appraisal system in your agency requires you to have meetings with the employee to discuss performance. Most plans will require at

---

* For a more complete discussion on the performance appraisal system including how to develop and write performance plans and how to counsel employees, see Performance Standards Made Simple!: A Practical Guide for Federal Managers and Supervisors, Second Edition, FPMI Communications, Inc. (1988).

least one meeting with each employee during the year and many managers meet with employees much more frequently than that to discuss the employee's progress in implementing the plan's requirements.

Early Meetings Head Off Trouble

If you are dissatisfied with an employee's performance, she should not be surprised by your dissatisfaction at the end of the rating period. As a supervisor, you have an obligation to meet with the employee and discuss any deficiencies in her progress before you attempt to take action. Waiting until the end of the year and surprising an employee is not a good idea, so begin dealing with potential problems as soon as possible.

In these early meetings, you should explain to the employee what is expected by the plan; any deficiencies in the employee's performance; and what is necessary to perform at an acceptable level. Take the time necessary to write down on the plan when you met with the employee. Also note the items discussed, suggestions for improvement, and how you

---

In meetings with the employee, you should discuss:

⊗ Requirements of the performance plan

⊗ Deficiencies in the employee's performance

⊗ What is necessary to perform the job successfully

77

offered to help the employee meet the requirements you have established.

Time to Improve

If your meetings with the employee do not result in improved performance, and the employee's performance on one or more critical elements is at the *unsatisfactory* level, the employee must be given a *formal opportunity period* in which to improve. This can be done at any time during the appraisal period or at the end of the rating cycle if you have rated the employee as being unacceptable.

The length of the time allowed to bring performance to an acceptable level will vary depending upon the nature of the work assignments. The minimum period is usually from 30 to 90 days. In some cases, the length of the period will be determined by a collective bargaining agreement that covers the employee.

During this *opportunity period*, you may give the employee special training assignments to improve his or her work, or other special action may be taken to attempt to improve the work to an acceptable level. As the supervisor, you will be the person primarily responsible for ensuring that the employee is given an opportunity to improve performance. For example, you may work more closely with the employee to ensure he understands the work assignments and how to complete them.

It is a good idea to make notes of any special efforts you make during this period. For example, if the employee is sent to a special training session, make a note of it in the employee's performance plan or in a separate memorandum. In the event that these special efforts are not successful, keeping track of them will be helpful in showing a third party that the agency met its obligation to help the employee improve his or her performance. This may play an important part in supporting any action you may take against the employee because of poor performance.

Options Available

As with disciplinary actions, a supervisor has several options available in the event the employee's performance does not improve to an acceptable level. These options are:

★ Reassignment

★ Reduction in Grade

★ Removal.

In deciding which option to exercise, you will want to consult with your personnel specialists. They can be helpful in letting you know which options are practical for a specific situation. For example, they can find out for you what other positions may be available in your organization for which the employee will qualify. Until you have this information, knowing whether a reassignment of the employee is possible will not be known.

If you decide there are no other jobs available for the employee at his or her current grade level, the agency should begin action either to reduce the employee's grade or to institute removal procedures.

Removing an Employee for Poor Performance

There are several steps involved in firing an employee for poor performance.

Removal Procedures

- Proposal issued
- Employee has right to respond
- Decision issued
- Action effected or terminated

Proposal

The proposal letter to the employee must be issued at least thirty days prior to the action being implemented. It must be signed by you or another supervisor having authority to sign a proposed removal action. This proposal will notify the employee of:

- The proposed action;

- The specific reasons for the proposal;

• The instances of unacceptable performance that occurred during the rating period;

• The critical elements of the performance plan that were not met by the employee;

• Right to representation by the union or other representative;

• The granting of reasonable time to answer the proposal orally or in writing.

Obviously, you will want to enlist the help of the personnel office in putting your letter together.

Final Decision

At the end of the notice period, a final decision will be issued after considering all of the facts in the case. The decision must be in writing and will notify the employee of the reasons for the decision, the effective date of the decision, and the appeal rights of the employee. Of course, if the decision is not to take the action, the employee will be notified of that decision and there would not be any effective date. The decision must usually be issued no later than 30 days after the notice period has expired.

Avenues of Appeal

Employees have the same avenues open to appeal a performance-based action as they do in appealing a severe disciplinary action. The most common avenues of appeal are to:

- The Merit Systems Protection Board;

- File a grievance under a negotiated grievance procedure;

- File an Equal Employment Opportunity complaint.

Before initiating any action based on performance, check with your personnel office and obtain their help. The personnel office will help you draft the proposal and decision letter including any appeal rights that a particular employee may have.

Key Points

★ Agency management can take a number of actions to correct unacceptable performance, including reassignment, training, reduction in grade, and removal.

★ Actions taken for unacceptable performance are handled much differently from disciplinary actions for unacceptable conduct.

★ The basic requirements for a performance-based action include a clear and specific performance plan for the employee, notice that the employee is not performing in one or more areas of the plan, counseling and assistance in an effort to help the employee's performance improve, notice of a proposed personnel action—such as reduction in grade or removal—provision of a specific time period for improvement, and a final decision.

★ Employees are entitled to appeal performance-based decisions to either the Merit Systems Protection Board or the Equal Employment Opportunity Commission, or under the negotiated grievance procedure contained in their labor agreement.

★ Assistance from the personnel office is essential in carrying out a performance-based action.

Handling Grievances And

Appeals

Handling Grievances and Appeals

There are several important things you need to realize before taking disciplinary action against an employee. First, no matter how good your reasons for taking the action, no matter how clear the facts and how correct the procedures used to carry it out, *the employee has the right to challenge the action by filing a grievance or an appeal.*

Managers sometimes miss this point, based on the belief that an employee must have a *good* reason to challenge an action before filing a grievance or an appeal. In reality, whether an employee has a solid basis for appealing your decision is something that is decided in dealing with the grievance itself. In other words, an employee can grieve or appeal first, and find out later if the complaint is legitimate.

A second important point to realize is that no matter how careful you are in putting together a disciplinary action, *there is a strong possibility it will be challenged through the grievance or appeal process.*

Why? For a variety of reasons, including the fact that employees often fail or refuse to admit to themselves—at least initially—that they may have done something wrong; because they think others have "gotten away with" similar behavior; because they think the punishment is too severe; or perhaps because the employee is simply hoping to get a lesser penalty or to avoid discipline altogether. Regardless of the reason, expect challenges to be filed to any disciplinary action you become involved in, and be pleasantly surprised if one is not filed.

The third important thing to bear in mind is that *you should not take such grievances and appeals personally*. Try not to view them as personal challenges to your authority, fairness or ability, although that may be hard to do if the employee says —as they sometimes do—harsh things about your judgment, fairness, or abilities as a manager or supervisor. Look at the entire process as part of doing business as a Federal manager, and not as a personal matter. This will make it easier to keep events in perspective and to avoid making remarks in anger that later can be used to make it appear you may have been biased against the employee. Remember, as the saying goes, "this too shall pass." When it does, in most cases you will still have to live with and get work done through the employee. The less damage done to your working relationship in responding to a grievance or appeal the better.

Your Role In Responding To Grievances And Appeals

If a grievance or appeal is filed on a disciplinary action you have taken or recommended, you may become involved in one or both of two ways. First, if a grievance is filed under a labor agreement, you may be required to answer the grievance at the first step of the procedure. Second, regardless of whether a contract grievance is filed or an appeal is made to the Merit Systems Protection Board or as a Equal Employment Opportunity Complaint, you may be required to take part in a hearing and give testimony on your reasons for taking or recommending discipline. Let's look at these two functions, one at a time.

Answering A Grievance

Under many labor agreements the grievance procedure provides that the first step for any grievance is with the immediate supervisor or, in some cases, with the first level of management with the authority to grant the grievance. If you are the person who recommended or ordered the disciplinary action, you may find yourself also reviewing the employee's grievance—which usually seeks to have your action overturned or reduced. This probably seems unusual and unnecessary, since by this time you will already have investigated the situation, proposed an action and heard the employee's response, and possibly made a final decision. And the chance that you missed something important or might want to change your mind is not likely. Nevertheless, that is the way the system sometimes works, so just do your best! Some grievance procedures recognize this and provide for filing the initial grievance regarding a disciplinary action with the next level above the person who made the decision to impose discipline.

When it is your responsibility to answer the first step grievance, the best thing to do is to take one more hard look at the facts, the points the employee raises, and your own reasoning to see if there is a basis for changing your mind. Then provide your answer with the best and clearest explanation you can put together.

More than likely, what will happen next is that the grievant and/or union will take the matter to the next step in the grievance procedure in an attempt to convince a higher level of management that the initial decision should be changed. At this point the grievance is no longer your direct responsibility. However, the grievance may be processed through all the steps in the grievance procedure, and may be taken to arbitration by the union. Or the employee may file an appeal through a statutory appeal process. If this occurs, you are likely to become involved in the arbitration or appeal process.

Testifying At a Hearing

Anytime you are involved in recommending or taking disciplinary action, you may later be called into a hearing to explain your reasons for the action. Although it is unlikely that you will look forward to these occasions, it is important to understand your role in the process and how it may affect you. Generally, there are three types of information that you will be asked to provide in any hearing of this kind.

★ **Providing background and factual information.**

When agency management disciplines an employee it must be prepared to present evidence to prove that the employee did something and that it was wrong to do so. Usually this means that the employee's supervisor is required to explain what happened (e.g., the employee came in to work smelling of alcohol), to explain what was said or what occurred during the event or incident, and finally, what resulted or might have resulted from the incident. Often it is also necessary to "set the scene" by providing a description of the workplace, what is done there, how it is done and who does the work. In other words, you may be asked to provide background information for the benefit of the arbitrator or the person hearing the grievance or appeal.

★ **Explaining how the behavior breaks rules or impacts on the organization, and your reasons for using discipline.**

To illustrate, if an employee failed to show up for an overtime work assignment, you would probably testify that he was assigned to work but failed to show up, and you will also testify as to the negative effect that this failure to work had—or could have had—on your operation. For example, if important work was not accomplished, if extra costs were incurred, or if an unacceptable example was set for other employees, you would explain how they were caused by the employee's actions. In hearings before the MSPB this is known as showing a "nexus," which is a legalistic way of saying that you are making a connection between the employee's conduct and the impact on your ability to accomplish the organization's work and mission.

★ **Explaining how and why you chose the specific disciplinary penalty imposed on the employee.**

Usually this requires that you explain what factors you took into account—such as the seriousness of the offense and its impact on your operation, the agency penalty guide recommendations for this kind of offense, and the employee's record—and how you concluded that the penalty you chose was reasonable in light of these factors.

Please note several things about the three kinds of information you may be required to provide. First, none of it should be unknown to you. These are all things you should know and be able to talk about without much trouble—especially if you have kept some memory jogger notes and use them to refresh your memory before you have to testify. Second, you will have considerable help in getting this information out at the hearing. A management representative will be there to ask you questions that will help you to remember and talk about all the items to be covered. The questions you will be asked and the answers you will provide usually be discussed with the representative before the hearing. Third, responding to these questions will not result in the dramatic ending of a Perry Mason thriller in which the witness suddenly confesses to murder, burglary or other mayhem.

The Role of the Management Representative

You will not be alone in providing information during the hearing. Your agency will furnish a representative to help you convey the information to the deciding official in a clear, convincing manner.

The management representative who helps you to present your story at hearing may be the same personnel specialist who helped you put together and process the disciplinary action. If so, the representative will already be familiar with the case.

Sometimes, however, the representative assigned to the case may be an attorney or someone else who was not directly involved in helping you to take the disciplinary action. In that case, you will have to work harder to make sure the representative fully understands what happened, the nature of your operation, and how the employee's actions affected it. In general, you can expect the management representative to do the following things:

★ **Understand all the important facts.**

Again, if the representative is already quite familiar with your operation and the case at hand, this will not be difficult. But if not, it is important for you to realize that you need to fill in the blanks to make sure that the representative has and understands all the important facts—such as where the employee and the supervisor fit into the chain of command, what specific work is done, and how it is done. Most representatives will meet and talk with you one or more times before the hearing to ask you questions that will help them understand the facts and gather necessary documents. Be patient and helpful. Remember, they do not know all that you do, and they are there for the sole purpose of helping you to explain your actions.

★ **Go over the specific questions you will be asked at the hearing.**

Although it may seem artificial, the way you and other witnesses are required to get their information across at a hearing is through a question and answer approach. That being the case, your representative will usually work closely with you to:

• Determine which information is most important to get on the record and

• What questions he will ask you to bring out the information.

★ **Prepare you for cross-examination.**

Despite its ominous sound, this usually is nothing more than going over the kinds of questions the opposing representative might ask and giving you advice on how to handle questions on cross-examination. For example, "If you do not know the answer to a question, you will probably be told "Do not try to guess,"; "Do not argue with the other representative," and similar words of wisdom.

Remember, in disciplinary cases the employee is always presumed innocent until proven guilty, so the agency must prove that the employee committed an offense, that it had a negative impact on the agency, and that the penalty is appropriate. If these points are not established, the agency's action will be overturned. What's the point? Simply this: it is extremely important for you to work closely with your management representative to make sure the facts and the reasons for taking the action are clearly presented. *If these are not presented in a clear, convincing manner, the action will be overturned.*

Key Points

★ Disciplinary actions can be, and usually are, grieved or appealed under established grievance or appeal procedures.

★ It is important to deal with grievances and appeals in a business-like manner, not taking the matter personally.

★ If the employee chooses to file a grievance under the labor agreement, you may be required to answer the grievance at the first step level.

★ Regardless of whether the employee files a grievance or an appeal, you may be required to participate in a hearing on the matter and to testify regarding background facts, the reasons you determined that discipline was necessary, and why you selected the specific penalty that was imposed.

★ It is important to work very closely with the management representative to make sure that all of the important facts and reasons for your actions are brought out clearly.

★ The management representative will work with you before the hearing to discover all the important facts, develop the questions that he or she will ask you at hearing, and to prepare you for cross examination by the opposing representative.

Practical
Advice

Practical Advice

As a supervisor, you have a responsibility to ensure that disciplinary action is taken when necessary to correct an employee's actions. Not taking any action often seems like the easiest path to follow for a Federal supervisor, even when experiencing difficulties with an employee. And, realistically, doing nothing is the easier, less painful course of action in the short run because it avoids conflict and confrontation.

But in the long run, failing to take disciplinary action will create more problems than it will solve and only evades the responsibility you accepted when you became a supervisor. As a Federal manager, you have to face the conflict, responsibility and tension that may come with imposing disciplinary action when necessary to correct the actions of one of your employees.

We have covered the basics you need to successfully take disciplinary action. The essence of any action boils down to this:

★ **Be fair** in your dealings with all employees.

★ **Be consistent** in your treatment of all employees.

★ **Know the facts** in a situation before acting.

★ **Use the support systems available to you** such as the personnel office and the advice and guidance of your fellow managers.

★ **Accept responsibility for making hard decisions** and taking the actions necessary to correct the problem.

Remember also that when you became a supervisor, no one said it would be easy. (If you were told that, you now know it was a lie!) Your greatest reward for being a good supervisor will be the intrinsic satisfaction that comes from knowing you have taken the steps necessary to have an efficient, effectively managed organization and that you have earned the respect of your peers and employees.

We hope that this book will be helpful to you in knowing if, when and how to take a disciplinary action.

Other Publications Available From FPMI Communications, Inc.

To order copies of any publications from FPMi Communications, call or send your order to:

FPMI Communications, Inc.
3322 South Memorial Parkway
Suite 40, Building 400
Huntsville, AL 35801
(205) 882-3042
Fax (205) 882-1046

FPMI publications include:

The Federal Manager's Guide to Discipline ($7.95)

Practical Ethics for the Federal Employee ($7.95)

The Federal Manager's Guide to TQM ($7.95)

Managing Leave and Attendance: A Guide for the Federal Supervisor ($7.95)

The Federal Manager's Guide to EEO ($7.95)

The Supervisor's Guide to Federal Labor Relations ($7.95)

The Desktop Guide to ULP's ($35.00)

The Federal Manager's Guide to Preventing Sexual Harassment ($7.95)

Sexual Harassment and the Federal Employee ($4.95)

The Federal Supervisor's Guide to Drug Testing ($7.95)

The Federal Employee's Guide to Drug Testing ($2.95)

Performance Standards Made Simple!: A Practical Guide for Federal Managers and Supervisors ($7.95)

The Bargaining Book: A Guide to Collective Bargaining in the Federal Government ($9.95)

The Union Representative's Guide to Federal Labor Relations ($8.95)

The Federal Labor & Employee Relations Update ($145.00)
(The *Update* is a monthly publication. The price is for a one year subscription.)

The Federal Manager's Edge ($38.00) (The *Edge* is a monthly newsletter specifically written for Federal managers.

The *MSPB Alert!* is a monthly bulletin of recent decisions of the Merit Systems Protection Board. The price is $125.00 per year or $35.00 per year if ordered in conjunction with the *Federal Labor & Employee Relations Update.*

Quantity discounts are available for all publications from FPMI Communications. For more information, please call or fax your request to us.

FPMI Training Seminars for Federal Supervisors and Managers

The Federal Personnel Management Institute, Inc. specializes in training seminars for *Federal* managers and supervisors. These seminars can be conducted at your worksite at a per person rate that is substantially less than open enrollment seminars.

Each seminar includes a copy of the appropriate book for each participant as well as a workbook including copies of all workshops and materials presented in the seminar.

The instructors for FPMi seminars have all had practical experience with the Federal Government and know problems Federal supervisors face and how to deal effectively with those problems. FPMi also conducts specialized training seminars for personnel practitioners as well.

Some of the seminar-workshops available from FPMi include:

"The Federal Drug Testing Program"

"Preventing Sexual Harassment"

"How to Take Effective Disciplinary Action"

"Managing Unionized Employees Effectively"

"How to Write Effective Performance Standards"

"Basic Labor Relations Workshop"

"Negotiations Workshop"

"Managing Labor Relations Conflict"

For more information contact FPMi at:

Federal Personnel Management Institute, Inc.
3322 South Memorial Parkway
Suite 40
Huntsville, AL 35801
(205) 882-3042

FPMI
Communications, Inc. Will Customize Our Books For Federal Agencies

FPMI Communications will customize any of our books to meet the specific needs of your agency. For example, if you would like to incorporate a specific policy or procedure unique to your agency or to include an introductory letter from the head of your agency or organization to all employees, this can often be quickly and easily incorporated.

Depending upon the extent of the changes necessary and the size of your order, this can often be done at little or no additional cost to your agency.

For more information on our book customizing program, call or write to FPMI Communications, Inc. at the address given on the title pages.